TAYLOR SWIFT

her story

UPDATED FAN EDITION

By Lexi Ryals & Grace Mack
Illustrated by Erwin Madrid

Scholastic Inc.

No matter what happens in life, be good to people. Being good to people is a wonderful legacy to leave behind.

—T.S.
(Taylor Swift)

Photo Credits

Photos ©: cover: VICTOR AUBRY/SIPA/Newscom; back cover: Album/Alamy Stock Photo; 2: John Shearer/TAS23/Getty Images for TAS Rights Management; 10: photo by TheFunTimesGuide.com; 13: Al Messerschmidt/Getty Images; 14 background: Gino's Premium Images/Alamy Stock Photo; 16: AP Photo/Nati Harnik; 19 center: Al Pereira/WireImage/Getty Images; 19 bottom: Marc Piasecki/FilmMagic/Getty Images; 22: Matt Sayles/Invision/AP; 24 top: Matt Winkelmeyer/TAS18/Getty Images for TAS; 24 center: Patti McConville/Alamy Stock Photo; 25: Gareth Cattermole/TAS18/Getty Images for TAS; 26 center: PjrStudio/Alamy Stock Photo; 26 bottom: PA Images/Alamy Stock Photo; 27: PA Images/Alamy Stock Photo; 28: Stephen Chung/Alamy Stock Photo; 29: Kevin Mazur/Getty Images for The Recording Academy; 30: Matt Winkelmeyer/Getty Images for dcp; 31: Hazel Plater/Alamy Stock Photo; 32 top left: Kevin Mazur/Getty Images for TAS Rights Management; 32 top right: Kevin Mazur/Getty Images for TAS Rights Management; 32 center: Kevin Mazur/Getty Images for TAS Rights Management; 33 bottom: Thomas Jackson/Alamy Stock Photo; 34: Allen J. Schaben/Los Angeles Times via Getty Images; 36: John Shearer/Getty Images for TAS; 37 center: New Line/Kobal/Shutterstock; 37 bottom: Universal Pictures/Moviestore/Shutterstock; 38 top right: Kevork Djansezian/Getty Images; 38 center: John Shearer/Getty Images for MTV; 39: AP Photo/George Walker IV; 40 bottom left: Thomas Jackson/Alamy Stock Photo; 40 bottom right: Abaca Press/Alamy Stock Photo; 41 top: Patrick Smith/Getty Images; 41 bottom: Patti McConville/Alamy Stock Photo; 42: Raj Valley/Alamy Stock Photo; 43: Album/Alamy Stock Photo; 44: Kevin Mazur/Getty Images; 45: Abaca Press/Alamy Stock Photo; 46: John Shearer/Getty Images for The Recording Academy; 47: AFF/Alamy Stock Photo. All other stock photos © Getty Images and Shutterstock.com.

This unauthorized biography was carefully researched to make sure it's accurate. Although the book is written to sound like Taylor Swift is speaking to the reader, these are not her actual statements. Portions of this book were previously published under the titles *When I Grow Up: Taylor Swift* and *Taylor Swift: Her Story*.

ISBN 979-8-225-06514-0

10 9 8 7 6 5 4 3 2 1 26 27 28 29 30

Printed in the U.S.A. 40

This edition first printing 2026

Book design by Cheung Tai

My name is Taylor Swift. I was born on December 13, 1989, in Reading, Pennsylvania. I grew up in a small town nearby, called Wyomissing, on a Christmas tree farm with my parents and my younger brother, Austin. My mom ran the farm and my dad worked for a financial company.

I've known I wanted to be a country music singer since I was around ten years old, when I got my first country music **album**, *Blue*, by LeAnn Rimes. I listened to it over and over until I had memorized every song. My parents encouraged my dream by enrolling me in singing lessons.

Another dream of mine was to perform onstage, so my parents signed me up for acting lessons, too. I starred as Sandy in a local production of the musical *Grease*. I also auditioned for different Broadway shows in New York City, which was only a bus ride away from my hometown. But I never got any of the parts I auditioned for.

Back home, I began to focus more on music. I started singing **karaoke** at local fairs and festivals when I was ten years old. I won several contests and even got to open a hometown show for country music legends the Charlie Daniels Band.

When I was eleven, I recorded my first **demo tape** of me singing my favorite country songs. My mom drove me down to Nashville, Tennessee, where many country music stars get their start, and I left my demo with all of the country **music labels**. Unfortunately, back then no one wanted to give me a **record deal**. But I wasn't about to give up on my dream!

In sixth grade, my friends decided they didn't like me anymore. They left me out of the group and made fun of me. It was awful! I learned to play guitar and started writing songs. I always turned to music when I felt sad, and it made me feel better to write down how I was feeling. I wrote one of my very first songs about those mean girls. It's called "The Outside."

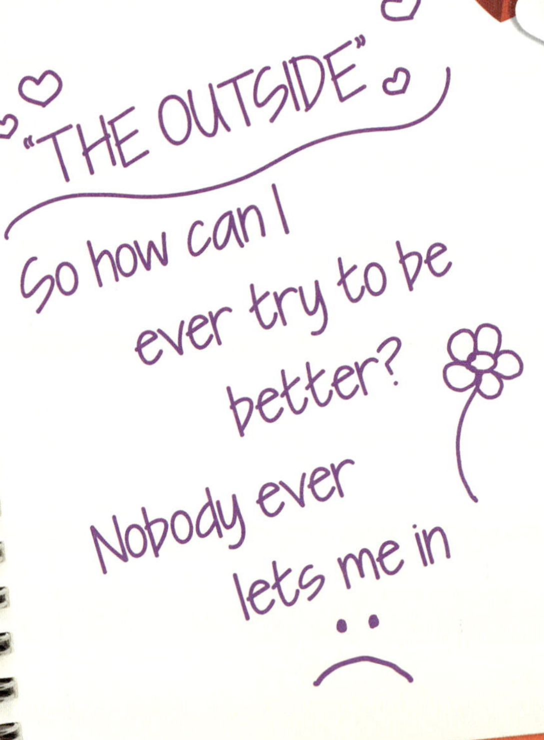

My family could see how serious I was about becoming a country music singer. I spent nearly all my time writing songs, singing, practicing guitar, and performing whenever I could. When a music label offered me a **development deal**, my whole family moved to Nashville. They've always supported my music dreams!

Unfortunately, my development deal didn't work out. The company wasn't interested in letting me write my own songs. I was disappointed, but it only made me more determined to write great songs and find the right label. I kept writing songs, and when I was fourteen, Sony offered me a job as a staff writer. I was the youngest writer they'd ever had!

When I was sixteen, I finally signed a record deal, with Big Machine records. I was so excited! The company brought in some of the best **producers** in country music to help me record my first album, *Taylor Swift*. They gave me lots of guidance, but they also listened to what I wanted. Recording in a professional music studio was really fun, but it was also a ton of work to juggle with high school!

Many people didn't think a teenager should record an album. They said no one would want to listen to songs about teenage problems. At the time, I felt like my record label believed in me. Since I'd been writing songs for four years, I had a lot of material to choose from! I'd written about my ex-friends, my first boyfriend, and having a crush on a boy who didn't know I liked him. My music came from my heart, and the feelings I sang about were familiar to other teens like me.

Luckily, lots of people (and not just teens) loved my music! Within a year, *Taylor Swift* went **platinum**. My first hit was "Tim McGraw," followed by "Teardrops on My Guitar." I got to go on tour as the opening act for different country music stars, including George Strait and Rascal Flatts. It was tough to balance music, high school, and friends, but it was worth it. I graduated with great grades, and I loved being on the road and getting to meet all my new fans.

I couldn't wait to record another album. My second album, *Fearless*, came out in 2008, when I was eighteen years old. I worked with other songwriters and producers, but I wrote most of the songs myself. Two of the most popular songs from *Fearless* were "Love Story" and "You Belong with Me." The album went platinum almost immediately—it was so cool! I went on a tour that took me all over the United States. It was my first time **headlining** a tour, and I had so much fun! I couldn't believe that my dreams of being a country music star were all coming true.

My third album, *Speak Now*, came out in 2010, when I was twenty-one years old. It debuted at number one and sold over six million copies! This was the first time I'd written every song on an album all by myself, so it meant a lot to me. I wrote about things that had actually happened in my life, including "Back to December," which was an apology to an ex-boyfriend, and "Mean," which was my way of telling a music critic to stop bullying me.

I went on my *Speak Now* world tour for almost two years, playing huge arenas around the globe. I'd never had the opportunity to travel to so many amazing places, and I loved getting to see famous landmarks and try foods that were new to me. It was exhausting, but so much fun. Luckily, I was able to take breaks between different parts of the tour so that I could rest, spend time with friends and family, and get back into the recording studio to work on my next album.

Red was my fourth album, and it was all about love. I'd had my heart broken a few times by then, so I used those experiences to write many of the songs, like "I Knew You Were Trouble" and "We Are Never Ever Getting Back Together." I worked with songwriters who focused on pop and alternative styles, so it had less of a country sound than my earlier albums. *Red* debuted at number one in October 2012 and was my fourth album to be certified **quadruple platinum**. I guess my fans liked it!

After headlining huge tours, releasing multiple albums, and winning some big awards, I was officially a star. One downside to being famous is that the media pays a lot of attention to me. I get photographed everywhere I go, and there are a lot of articles written about what I'm wearing or who I'm dating. It's nice that my fans want to know all about me, but sometimes people say things that are untrue or that really hurt my feelings. Mostly, I try to ignore those stories and focus on my music and my fans.

My fans are the best part of being a star. I love meeting them at shows and events. But my favorite thing to do is to totally surprise a fan. For example, I went to prom with one fan for a show on MTV. I also leave comments on fans' websites, blogs, and social media pages. One time, I took a car full of toys to a fan's home for her son after hearing she was having a hard time. I even photobombed a fan's family picture session in a Nashville park! Seeing the look on fans' faces when I surprise them is priceless. And getting to hear how my music has affected them means the world to me.

After four successful albums and three major tours, I decided it was time to change things up. I wrote a lot of new songs on the *Red* tour, and I realized that none of them were country songs. I was inspired by pop music and was ready to record my very first pop album! So I found the best pop songwriters and producers in the music industry and convinced them to work with me. I spent most of 2014 writing, recording, and experimenting with my new sound—and it really paid off.

I released my fifth album, *1989*, in October 2014, and I was so nervous that I barely slept the night before it went on sale! I didn't have to be worried, though, because my fans loved it. The album sold more than 1.2 million copies the week it went on sale, making it my most successful release yet (at that time). Everyone embraced my new sound in songs like "Shake It Off" and "Blank Space." I am so glad that I trusted my instincts and tried something new. Fear should never hold you back from taking a risk!

I wanted my *1989* tour to be really special and different from my previous tours. I had lots of new fans who love pop music, and I even had a new band for the occasion. I'd been feeling inspired by Broadway shows, so I wanted my *1989* tour to have lots of big sets. I love surprising my audience whenever I can with special guests and new songs. I wanted this to be my best tour yet!

When *1989* came out, my career was going better than ever, but with that success and fame also came negative attention. There were more mean things said about me than ever before, especially on the internet, and it was hard for me to deal with hearing and reading all of it. Online bullies can be really cruel! I was feeling very low and decided to take some time to myself by moving to a new home and staying away from social media for a while.

While I was off social media, I spent time with family, friends, and loved ones, and I also worked on the music for my next album. I was inspired by electropop, R&B, and hip hop, as well as the bullying and media scrutiny I'd dealt with, when I made my sixth album, *reputation*. Some of the songs, like "Look What You Made Me Do," were also inspired by the hit TV show *Game of Thrones*. It debuted at the top of the Billboard 200 and sold 1.2 million copies in its first week on sale in 2017. *Reputation* was also my last album with the Big Machine label.

In 2018, I went out on a stadium tour for *reputation*. The tour was so big, it broke records! Netflix also released a **concert film** of the *reputation* tour. And that wasn't the only thing I was working on while on tour—the **documentary** *Miss Americana*, which came out on Netflix in January 2020, features footage from the *reputation* tour, too.

Miss *Americana* also shows me working on some of the songs and music videos for my seventh album, *Lover*, which came out in 2019. It was my first album released by Republic Records, and I wrote a lot of the songs about love, including love for my mother, who was sick when I wrote "Soon You'll Get Better." The whole album is really a love letter to love itself.

Around the same time *Lover* came out, the label I'd worked with on my first six albums was sold to a music manager who was a big bully. I'd been trying to buy my **master recordings** of those six albums back for years, and now they were owned and controlled by someone I did not get along with. I was mad and sad, and I started to form a plan: I would re-record my first six albums and release them all over again, with subtle changes to the old songs. I added new songs, too, so that I would own them once and for all.

In 2020, when the whole world was locked down during the COVID-19 pandemic, I used the time at home to keep working on new music. In July 2020 and December 2020, I released *folklore* and *evermore*, my eighth and ninth albums. I felt inspired by watching movies while I was quarantined at home, and I used my imagination to create intersecting characters and stories in the songs on *folklore*, like "Cardigan," "Betty," and "August." *Folklore* was my first surprise album, announced only a few hours before its release, and it was the bestselling album of 2020!

The success of *folklore* inspired me to keep imagining and playing with the same musical style, which led to the surprise release of *evermore* just a few months later. It felt really good for me to get creative in a new way, writing stories that weren't about my personal life into my songs. My time working on *evermore* overlapped with my re-recording of *Fearless*—I even recorded "Happiness" from *evermore* and "You Belong With Me (Taylor's Version)" from *Fearless (Taylor's Version)* on the same day!

FAVORITE POP ALBUM

TAYLOR SWIFT
"RED (TAYLOR'S VERSION)"

I released my first two re-recorded albums in 2021—*Fearless (Taylor's Version)* and *Red (Taylor's Version)*. Both re-recorded albums featured new songs, like "Message in a Bottle" on *Red (Taylor's Version)* and "Mr. Perfectly Fine" on *Fearless (Taylor's Version)*, as well as new versions of the original songs, like a ten-minute version of "All Too Well" on *Red (Taylor's Version)*. They both sold more copies than the original versions of the albums did, so I guess people liked the new and updated songs a lot!

Then, in 2022, I released my tenth studio album, *Midnights*, as well as *Midnights (3am Edition)*, which had seven extra songs on it. *Midnights* was inspired by thirteen different times I had been up in the middle of the night over the course of my life. Sleep is important, but some great songs came out of those sleepless nights! The first single from *Midnights*, "Anti-Hero," was the top-selling song of 2022, and *Midnights* was the top-selling album of the year, too. And it won the Grammy for Album of the Year!

Because of the COVID-19 pandemic, I hadn't been on a tour for an album since 2018, and I'd released four brand-new albums since then, plus the new music on my re-recorded albums! So in 2023, I set out on the biggest world tour I've ever done: The Eras Tour. It was a **retrospective** tour of my whole career, featuring songs from at least nine of my ten albums. I started training six months before the first show to prepare. Each show lasted over two hours, and included over 40 songs, almost as many dance numbers, and 16 costume changes. Whew!

It was worth all that work to put on a great show for my fans. I wanted to show them that I celebrate who I have been, who I am now, and who I will be—and that they should do the same—by taking them on a tour through the many different stages of my career. And the fans really showed up! The Eras Tour was the first music tour to earn over a billion dollars. I loved seeing my fans singing and dancing along, trading friendship bracelets with my song lyrics on them.

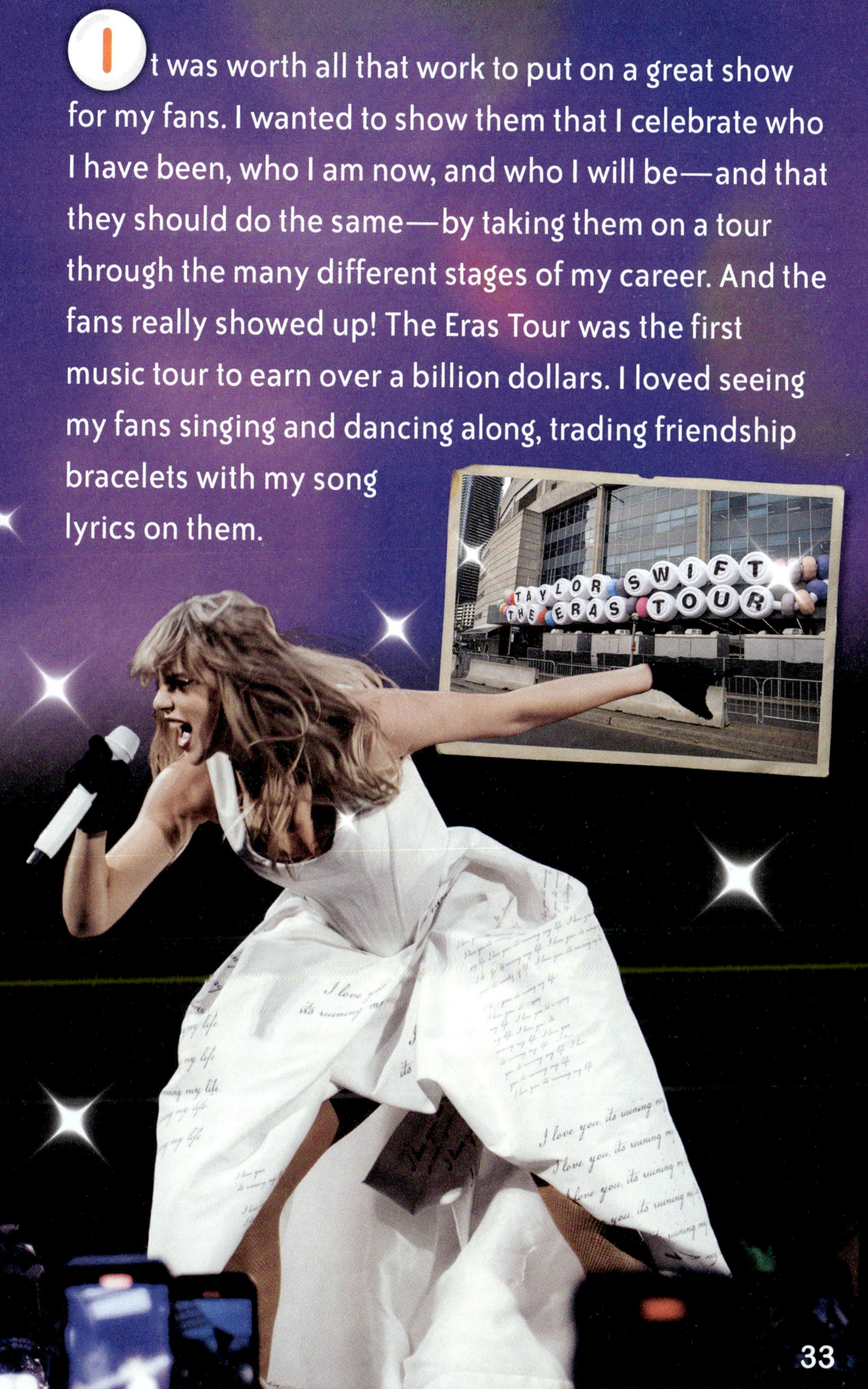

I had to build rest into my Eras Tour schedule, too, because those shows were hard and tiring. After performing a few shows in a row, I would rest for a full day. I only got out of bed to get food and then I would bring it back to bed and eat it there! It was fun to eat in bed and relaxing to rest all day — and it was also important for me to rest so I could give it my all during such an intense show.

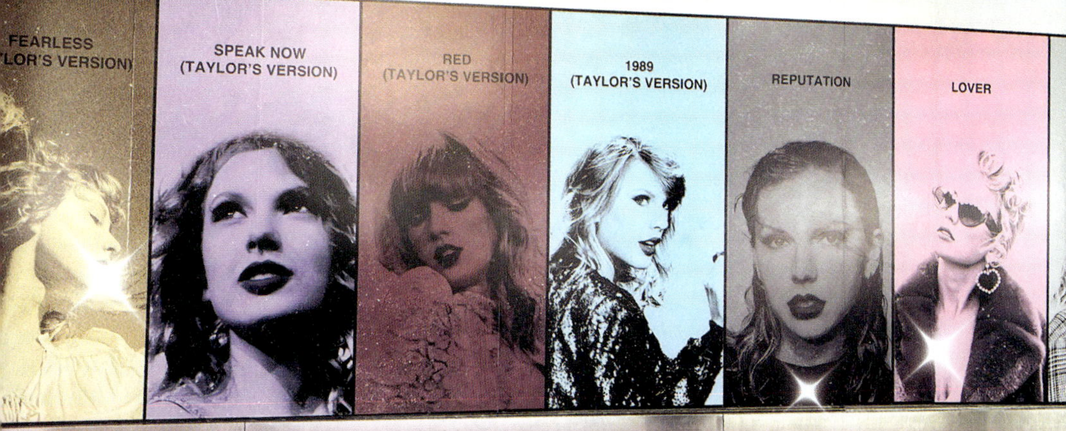

In 2024, my Eras Tour era officially came to an end. The last Eras Tour show was in Vancouver, British Columbia, on December 8, 2024, just a few days before my thirty-fifth birthday. In total, I performed 149 shows in fifty-one cities across five continents. The tour made over $2 billion in ticket sales, which is double the ticket sales of any concert tour ever. In May 2024, I updated the show a little to include songs from the album I released in April, *The Tortured Poets Department*.

The Eras Tour was a huge amount of work—and every drop of sweat was worth it.

Even though it's over, the Eras Tour will always live on in my heart—and on our screens! In October 2023, I released a concert film in theaters. The AMC movie theater chain had its highest ticket sales in one day when *Taylor Swift: The Eras Tour* movie tickets went on sale, and Beyoncé came to the premiere, which was so cool! The movie brought the tour to fans who weren't able to come see it in person. In July and October 2023, I also released my next two re-recorded albums: *Speak Now (Taylor's Version)* and *1989 (Taylor's Version)*. I worked really, really hard in 2023!

In addition to making music and performing, I've also been able to try acting, which is so much fun! I've hosted *Saturday Night Live*, had **cameos** and roles in *New Girl*, *Valentine's Day*, *The Giver*, *Amsterdam*, and more. I played an animated character when I recorded the voice of Audrey in *The Lorax* and got to play one of my favorite animals—a cat!—in the 2019 film adaptation of the musical *Cats*. (I went to "cat school" to prepare for that role!) I've moved behind the camera, too, by directing some of my music videos, as well as the short film for the ten-minute version of "All Too Well."

It always feels great when other people love my music, and I feel honored each time I win a new award. So far, I've won fourteen Grammy Awards, forty American Music Awards, multiple Country Music Association Awards and Academy of Country Music Awards, forty-nine Billboard Music Awards, thirty MTV Video Music Awards, and more, including a Primetime Emmy Award! Another way my work has been honored is that some college professors, including one at Harvard, have taught classes about my music! It's pretty cool to think of my lyrics being compared to classic poetry. I wonder if I'd ace that class if I took it . . .

One of the biggest honors I've ever received came near the end of 2023, when *Time* magazine named me Person of the Year. When they called to tell me, I asked if I could bring my cat to the photoshoot (they said yes, so my cat was with me on the cover of *Time*!). I'm so grateful to *Time* for the honor, and to everyone who made 2023 possible—especially my fans.

Another huge moment came during the 2024 Grammys. I won two awards, including Album of the Year—the fourth time I've received that honor. It was a record! I was so grateful that I made a surprise announcement about the release of my next album.

The Tortured Poets Department, my eleventh album, came out on April 19, 2024. It helped me get a lot of my feelings and recent heartbreak out into song. I started working on *The Tortured Poets Department* right after I turned in *Midnights*—sometimes I just can't stop writing songs!—and I kept on writing during the Eras Tour. The video for "I Can Do It With a Broken Heart" even features behind-the-scenes footage from the Eras Tour. When *TTPD* came out, it broke streaming records with over 300 million Spotify streams in one day, all thanks to my amazing fans (like you!).

In 2023, I started dating a professional football player named Travis Kelce. We both work demanding schedules, but we made time for each other even while I was touring and he was in the middle of the NFL season. I was able go to the Super Bowl in 2024 and 2025 to cheer on Travis and his team, the Kansas City Chiefs!

In August 2025, Travis and I announced our engagement on Instagram. We're getting married! As I once told my friend Selena Gomez, real love happens sometimes. I *still* believe that!

Remember when I started re-recording and re-releasing all of my older music so that I could officially own those songs? Well, in 2025, the day I'd dreamt of finally arrived: I reached a deal to make sure that all of my music, ALL OF IT, finally belongs only to me. It's hard to describe how happy this achievement has made me (when I try, I start crying happy tears)! I owe a giant THANK YOU to my family, friends, and fans, whose support and enthusiasm for the re-recorded "*(Taylor's Version)*" albums and the Eras Tour made it possible.

I know what you're wondering: now that I own all my master recordings again, will I still re-record and release *reputation (Taylor's Version)* and *Taylor Swift (Taylor's Version)*? The answer to that is complicated! I'm not so sure about re-recording and re-releasing *reputation*, though I'll probably release the vault tracks from that album one day. I've already re-recorded my debut album and I love how it sounds. There will be a right time for those two albums to find their way into the world, but for now, I'm celebrating the win of FINALLY owning ALL my music!

I've spent a lot of time on tour since my career started, and I'll likely go on more tours before my career is over. I've been lucky to have talented musicians perform with me, including Ed Sheeran, Florida Georgia Line, Ice Spice, Phoebe Bridgers, HAIM, Sabrina Carpenter, and more. My favorite thing about being on tour is getting to meet my fans in so many different places and hear their stories. I try to meet as many as I can—even if it means signing autographs for hours!

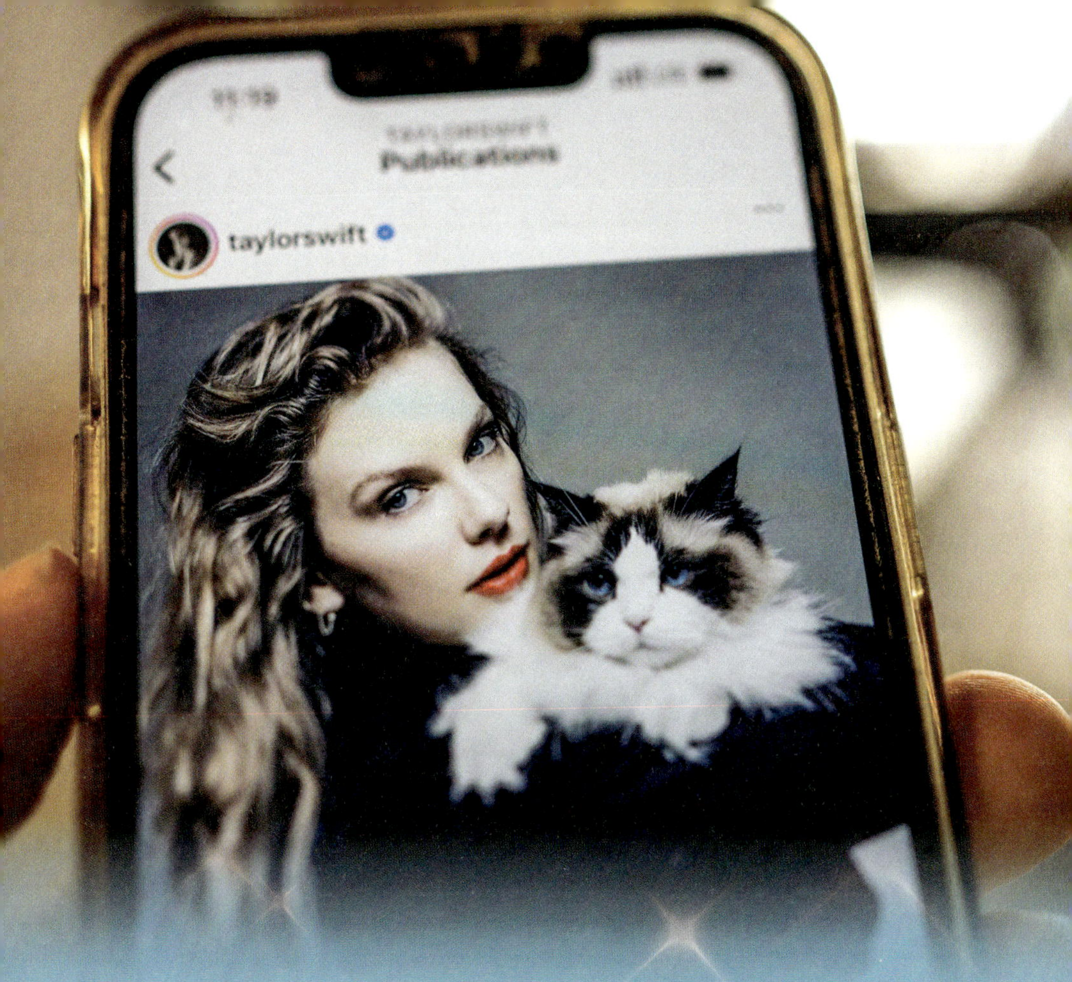

As much as I love being on the road, it's always nice to come home after a long trip. When I'm not working, I like to spend time with my friends, family, and my three cats, Meredith Grey, Olivia Benson, and Benjamin Button. Some of the things I love to do are cooking and baking (especially sourdough bread!), sewing, and crafting, like when my friends and I crafted homemade snow globes. My other passions include reading and hunting for antiques.

I've done *a lot* over the course of my career, and in August 2025, I added one more thing to that list: I made my first appearance on a **podcast**! Travis and his brother, Jason Kelce, had me on as a guest on their podcast, *New Heights*, and I announced my twelfth album: *The Life of a Showgirl*, out on October 3, 2025. The episode broke the Guinness World Record for most viewers watching a live stream at the same time.

I worked on *The Life of a Showgirl* while I was on tour, which was exhausting but exciting, too. It features twelve tracks (including one featuring my friend Sabrina Carpenter). I can't wait for the world to hear it.

So, what's next for me? I plan to keep doing more of what I love: writing songs, recording music, touring, and working with other talented musicians. My job is better than I ever imagined it would be when I was a kid. I'm so thankful that I get to live out my dream by performing and making music every day, and I can't wait to see what the future will bring!

GLOSSARY

ALBUM: a long recording on a record, CD, or digital download that usually includes a set of songs

CAMEO: a small role in a movie, play, etc., that is performed by a well-known star

CONCERT FILM: a filmed version of a concert performance that is edited and released like a movie

DEMO TAPE: a recording that shows what a performer can do

DEVELOPMENT DEAL: when a music label promises to develop a musician's skills and image before committing to recording an album

DOCUMENTARY: a movie, TV, or radio program that uses real-life footage to provide a factual record of events

HEADLINING: being the main performer in a show or concert

KARAOKE: a form of entertainment in which people take turns singing popular songs into a microphone over prerecorded music

MASTER RECORDING: the original recording of a song, sound, or performance

MUSIC LABEL: a company that produces musical recordings and represents musical artists and bands

PLATINUM: an award that is given to a singer or musical group for selling at least one million copies of a record

PODCAST: a music or talk program available as an audio file (sometimes with accompanying video) for download on the internet

PRODUCER: someone who is in charge of making and usually providing the money for a play, movie, or record

QUADRUPLE PLATINUM: an award that is given to a singer or musical group for selling at least four million copies of a record

RECORD DEAL: a contract between a musician or band and a music label in which they agree to record and produce an album

RETROSPECTIVE: of or relating to past events or situations